HAPPILY ABUNDANT INCREDIBLY RAMBUNCTIOUS

DeJa Clift

Koi Clift

Happily Abundant Incredibly Rambunctious
COPYRIGHT 2023 BY DEJA CLIFT
ALL RIGHTS RESERVED ISBN 979-8-9895498-0-1
NO PORTION OF THE BOOK MAY. REPRODUCED OR UTILIZED IN ANY FORM OR BY ANY MEANS - ELECTRONIC OR MECHANICAL. INCLUDING PHOTOCOPYING OR RECORDING OR BY ANY INFORMATION STORAGE AND RETRIEVAL SYSTEM - WITHOUT PERMISSION FROM THE AUTHOR

You are magic

Pssst
look throughout this book for magical hair tools and stay
til the end to find affirmations and definitions about
Black hair

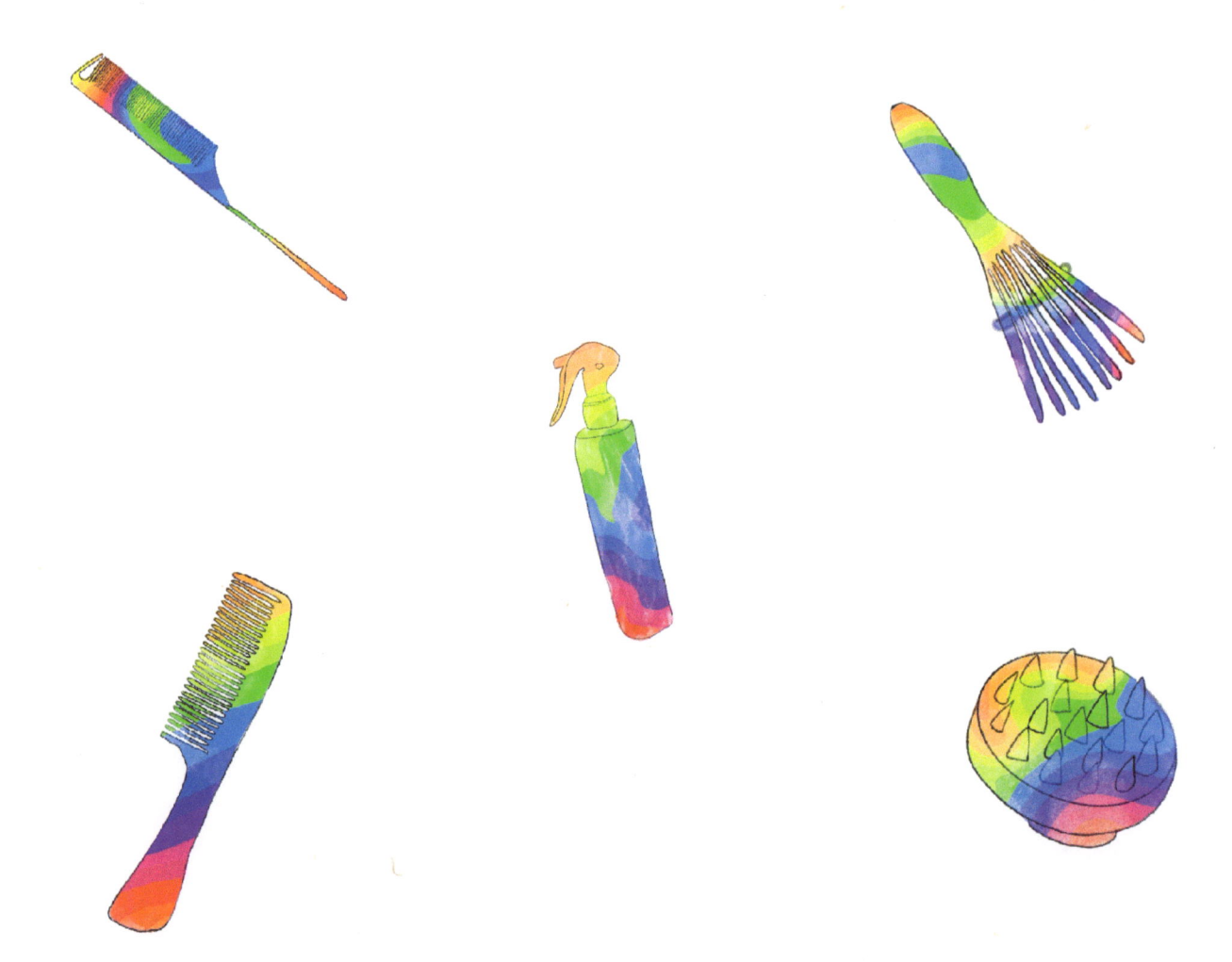

This book is dedicated to my son Koi, I love doing your hair every night. You are every good thing in the world, you are courageous and confident and I hope you keep joy in your life always

& Mom

I start each day with affirmations.

> I am creative inside and out. I am brave inside and out. I am courageous inside and out. I am beautiful inside and out. I am bigger than any challenge I face. I move in love because I am love and love flows through me.

Mama always told me my hair was beautiful.

If it was getting in my eyes or down to my thighs.

Sometimes I wonder, did my mom know how much people would talk about my hair when I was a baby? Did she know my hair would be different?

My sister and brother have different hair than me. My sister has short hair, hey girls can have short hair too!

My brother has long loose curls. Everyone loves him and wants his autograph. He's fashion all the time.

My dad is white and he has short hair and that's how he likes it

I used to wonder if I was supposed to wear my hair like this?

????

???? ????

My mom is Black & Indigenous
and she has different hair often.

I never know if she'll pick me up
from school with pink hair
or a HUGE Afro!

My mom is so cool. I love how she expresses herself with her hair.

I started to wonder how I could be just as brave with my hair.

Mama told me our people got their strength from their hair.

In our culture men have long hair.

To me my hair was magic.

You look like a girl
Are you a girl?   Are you sure?
You should cut your hair!

Then I got teased so much at school that I wanted to cut my hair. Every day I was called a girl.

That made me so sad and then I called my cousin. He's a teenager and has long hair!

He told me that I can't let bullies take my strength and boy or girl is not determined by length.

Many of my cousins have long hair. They even had long hair when they were my age!

My cousins are all so unique with their locs and fades. I love them.

I realized I'm beautiful, soft, and a warrior with my long hair!

My hair is not only my culture, it's my power and I will never let anyone dim my shine.

Mama said the minute I let someone else determine my worth I've lost.

Since you're looking at a winner I'm reclaiming every second I let anyone define me.

Because I can be anything and do anything! People's feelings about me are not my own. I know I am amazerrific.

I am me. Every strand of my hair is the link between myself and my strength.

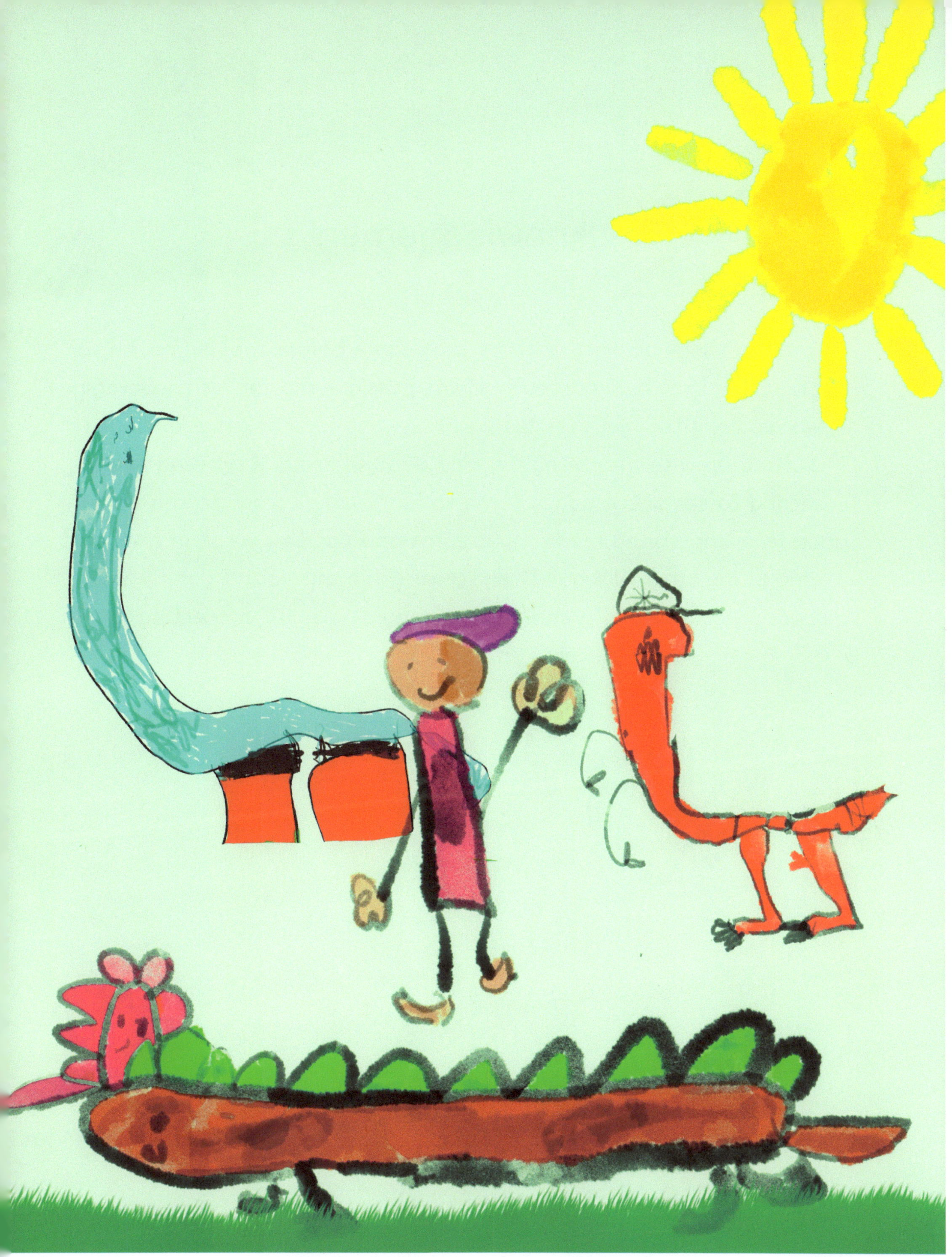

Acknowledgements:

I want to thank all Black authors that came before me! My cousin for showing me that being an author was possible and for his encouraging words along the way. Thanks Justin. I want to thank my family for putting up with me taking my iPad everywhere and drawing every second to see these pages come to life. Lastly, I want to thank my ancestors who visited me in my dreams and put this vision in my heart and in my head, without their stewardship and faith I don't know where I would be. My grandmothers prayers are still protecting me, I will carry on her legacy forever.

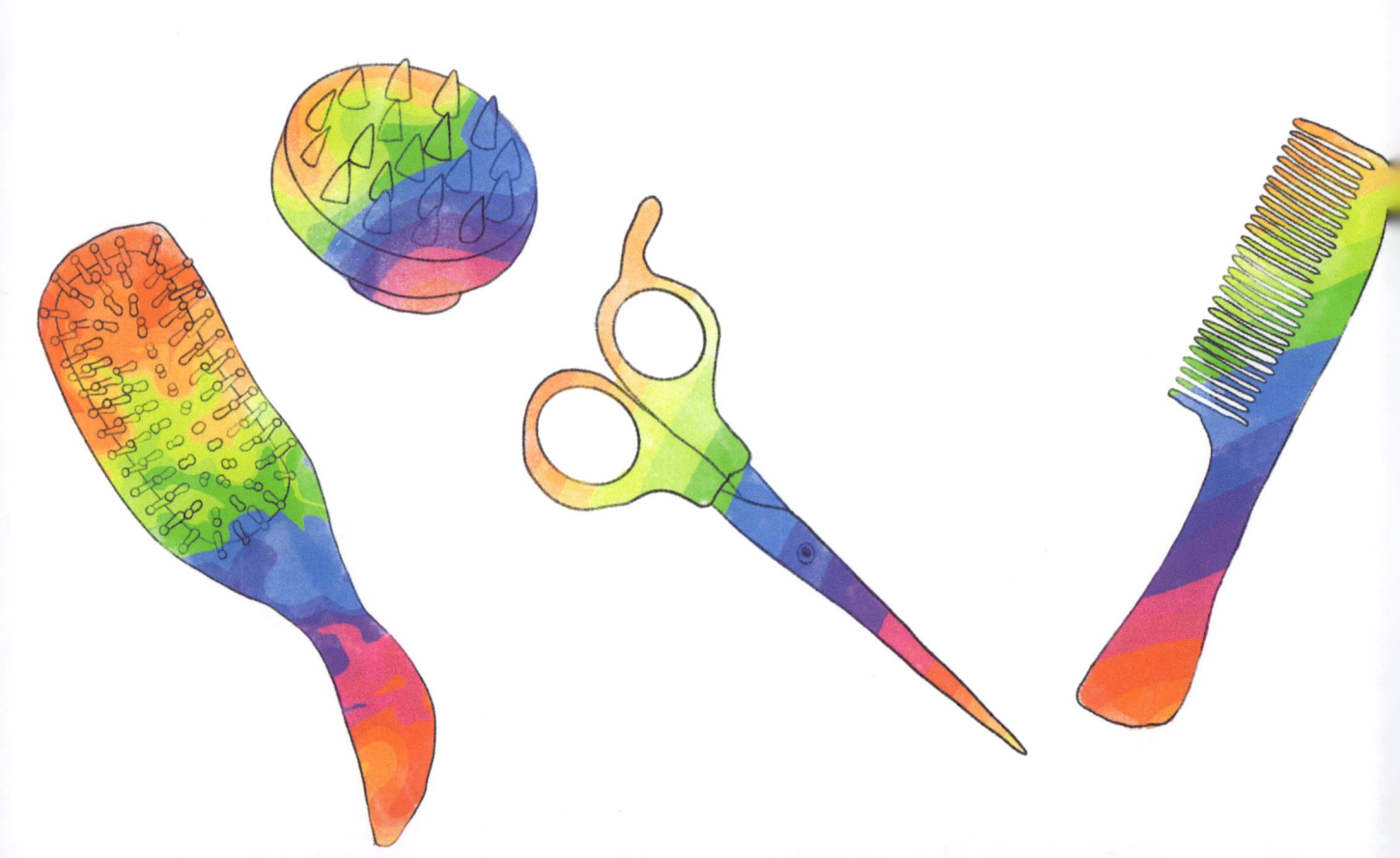

Affirmations

I am creative inside and out.

I am brave inside and out.

I am courageous inside and out.

I am beautiful inside and out.

I am bigger than any challenge I face.

I move in love because I am love and love flows through me.

I choose my own destiny.

I never give up until the job is finished.

I do my best always.

Black Hair The More You Know

Protective style - A hairstyle that puts the ends of hair away from being exposed to natural elements, such as sun and heat, and also constant manipulation through styling. Different protective styles include, but are not limited to twists, braids, wigs, cornrows, and locs.

Braids - There are many types of braids, including, but not limited to micro braids, two strand, and box braids. Braids can be individual and free flowing down. They can also be braided close to the scalp.

Waves - A close-to-the-scalp style that protects and arranges short, wavy-to-coily hair in a spiral wave pattern.

Locs - A hairstyle in which the hair is coiled onto itself and remains that way, thus "locking" and creating rope-like strands. When creating locs, people don't uncoil their hair. Locs can be made by braiding and twisting the hair into a specific style. They can be styled in many ways including updos, braids, and twists.

Hair texture - Texture refers to how thick each individual strand of hair is. Today's products describe textures on a scale of "fine" to "coarse." Curl type or pattern - The curl type is determined by the shape of the follicle of the hair. Most people with curlier hair have more than one type of pattern. There are sub-categories from A to C, which is based on the width of the curl, where A has the widest pattern and C is the smallest pattern. Hair type - Type 1 is straight, Type 2 is wavy, Type 3 is curly, and Type 4 is coily.

Detangle - The process of separating curls and coils from one another to prevent them from locking or becoming unkempt. The process involves combs, brushes, water, fingers, oils, and hair products.

Edges - The hairs along a person's front-facing hairline. Baby Hair - Short, fine, straight-to-wavy hairs along a person's hairline. Black women created the trend of styling these hairs into appealing swirls using small brushes.

Printed in the USA
CPSIA information can be obtained
at www.ICGtesting.com
JSHW040322131223
53650JS00002B/3